In this FIRST edition of The Most Relaxing Fashion Coloring Book you will find:

3 illustrations of the best photos from the Fashion Editorial "De Regreso al Campo"

3 illustrations of the best photos from the Fashion Editorial "Una Inusual Despedida"

2 illustrations of our best photos taken on San Juan Moda

2 illustrations of our best photos taken on West Fashion Week

5 original and unique fashion related illustrations

Created by Lourdes Martínez for
traffic‑chic

Illustrated by Sofía Carrasquillo

COPYRIGHT 2021 TRAFFIC CHIC
www.traffic-chic.com
Youtube: TRAFFIC CHIC

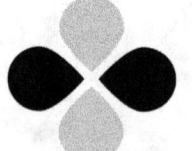

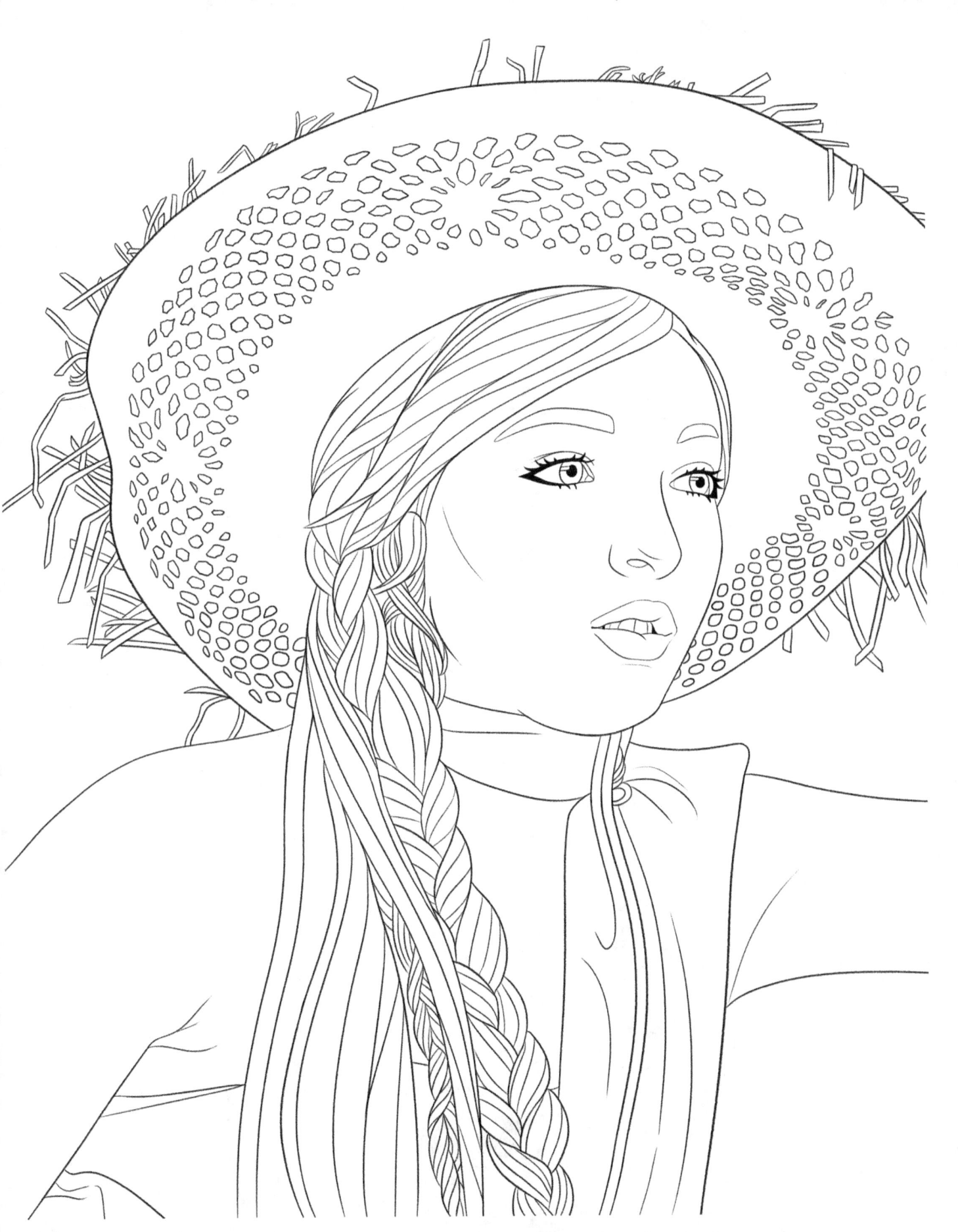

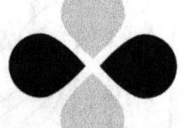

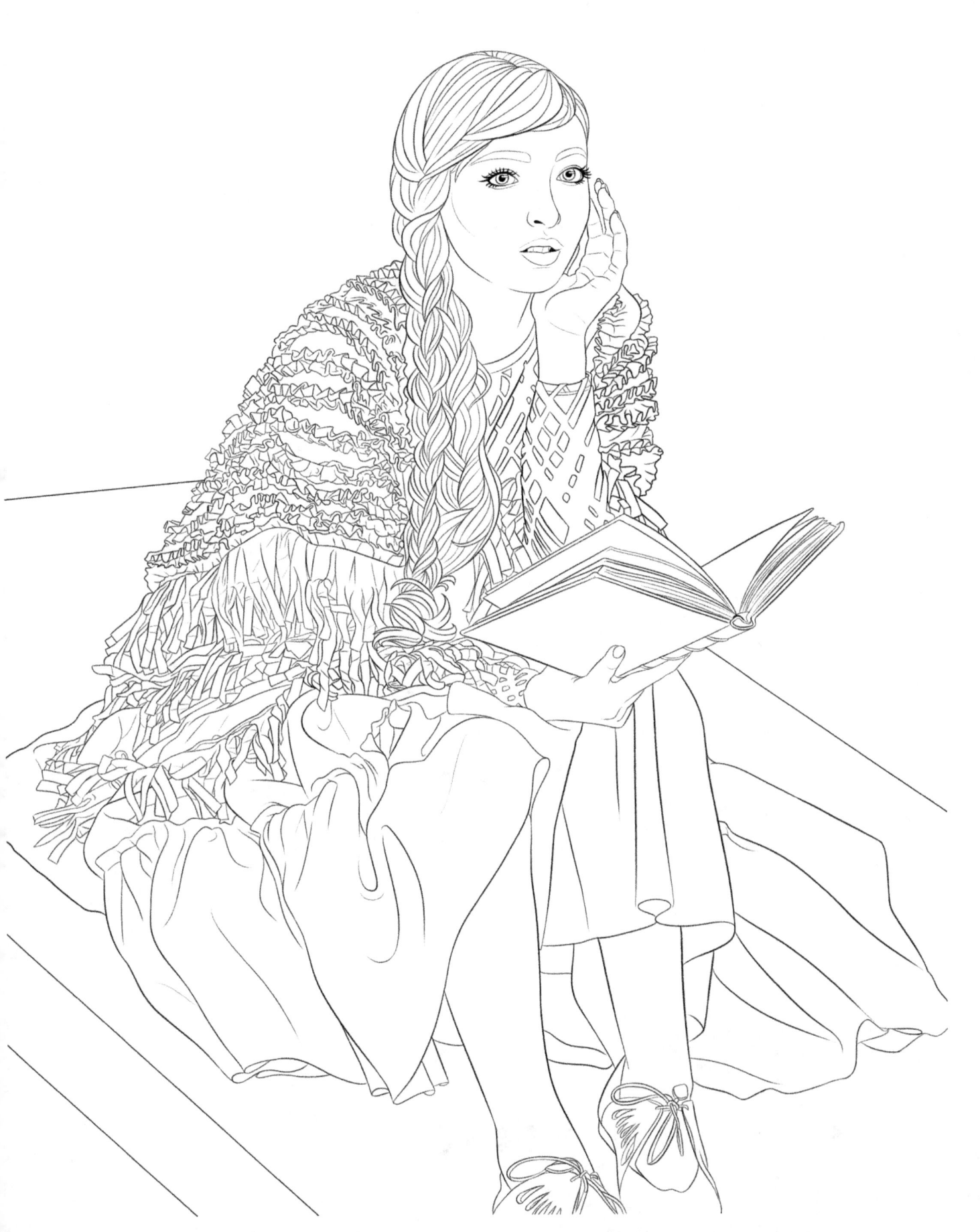

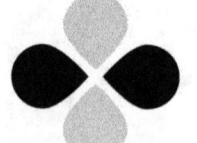

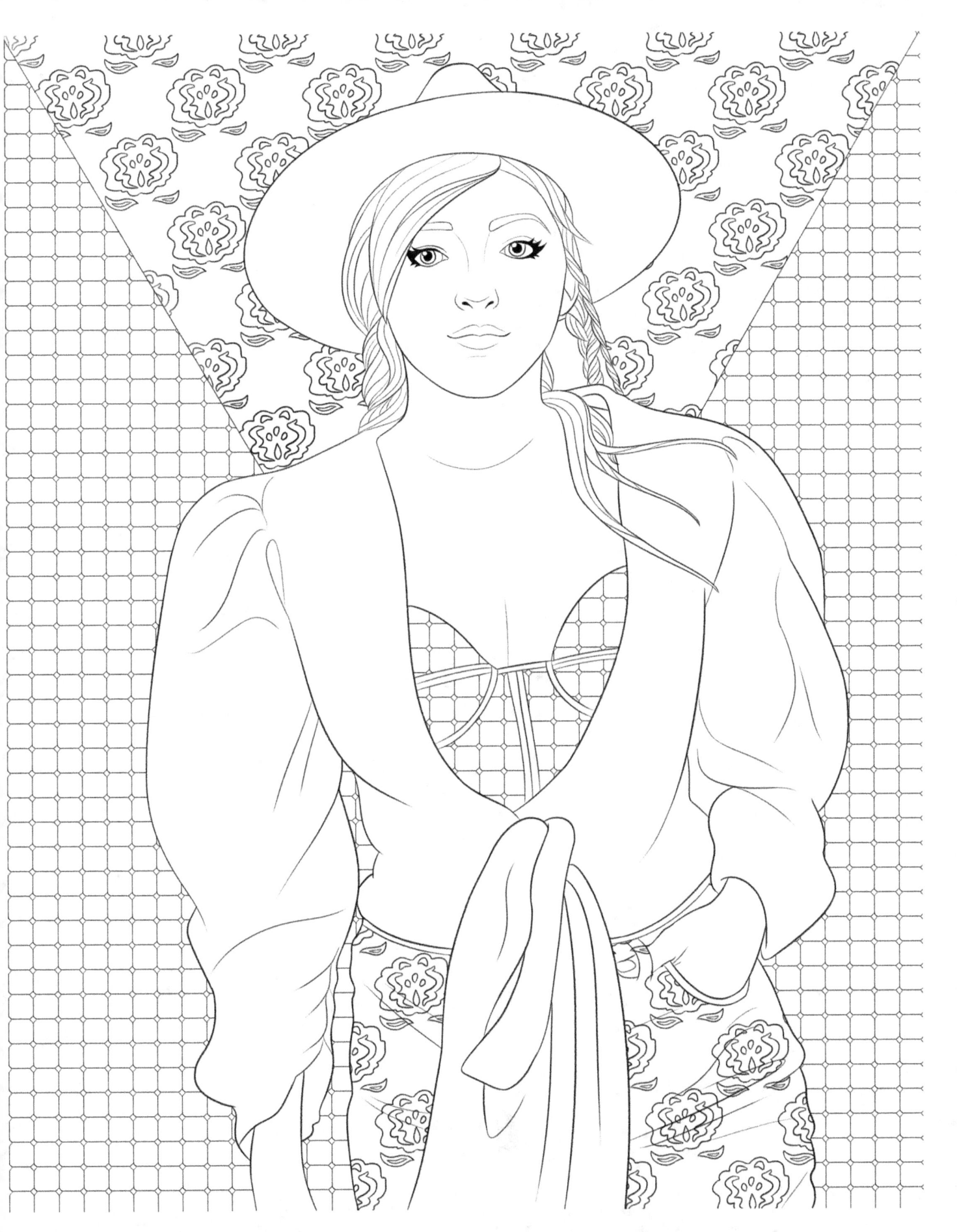

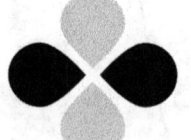

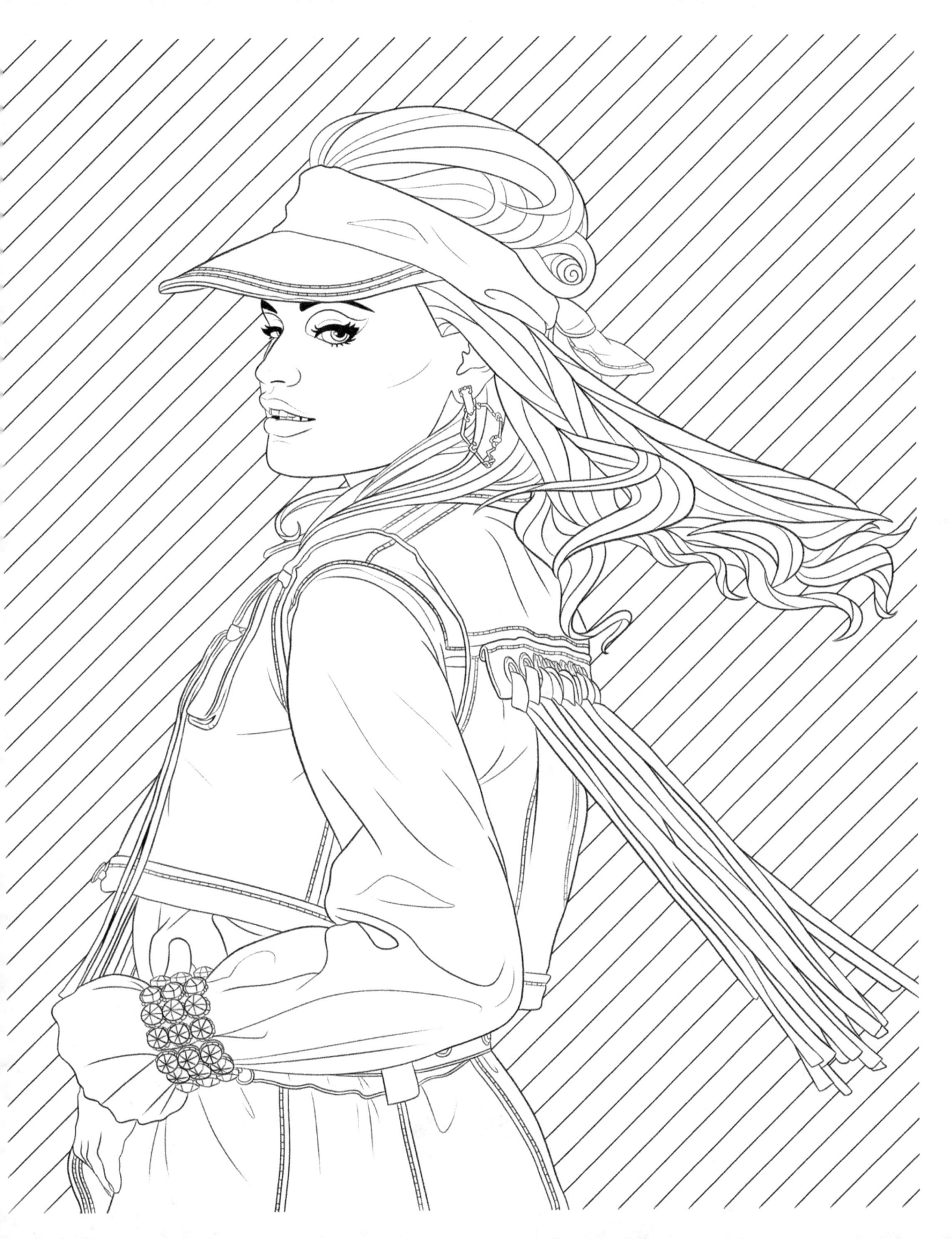

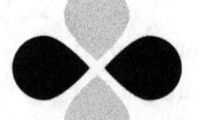

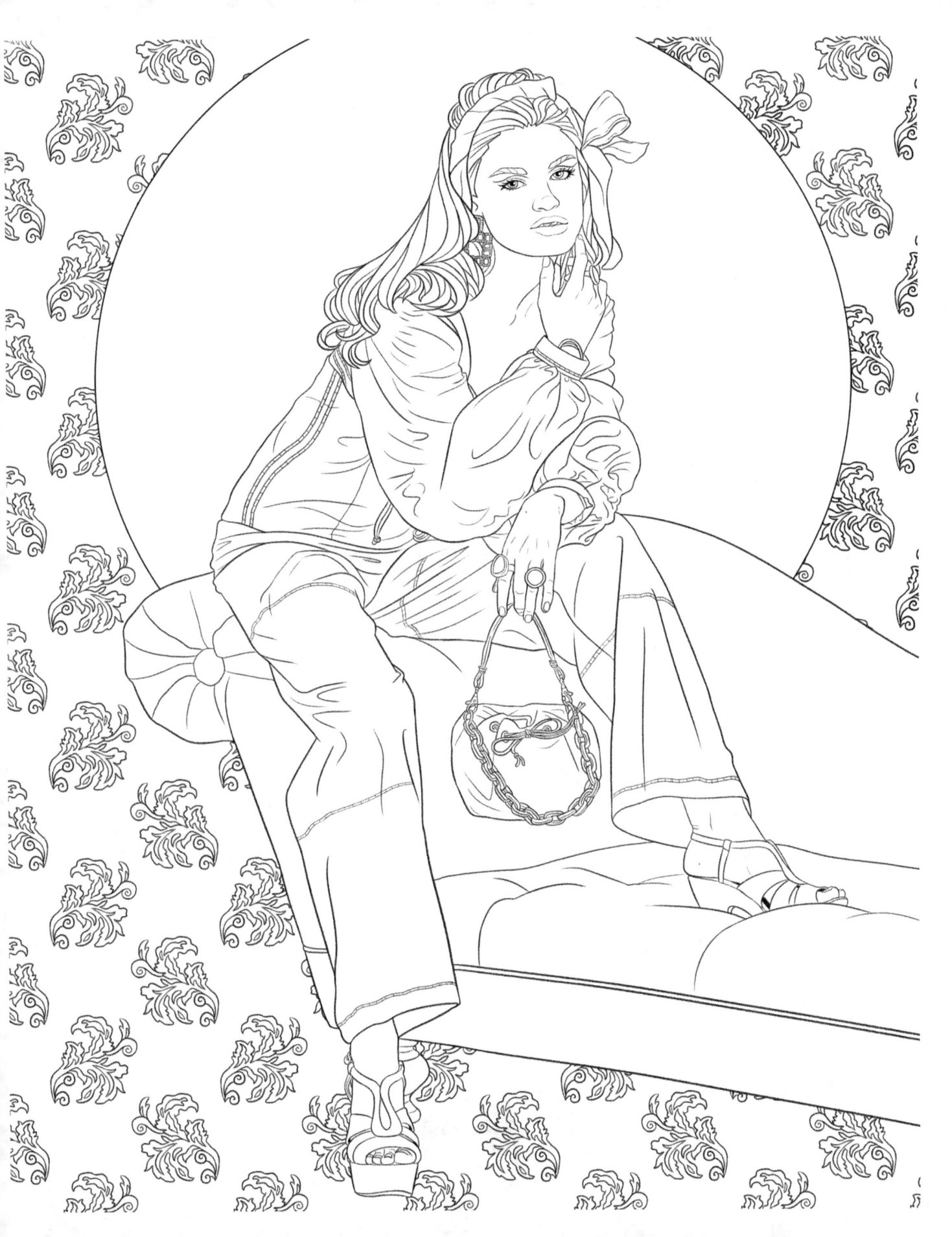

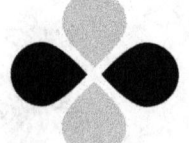

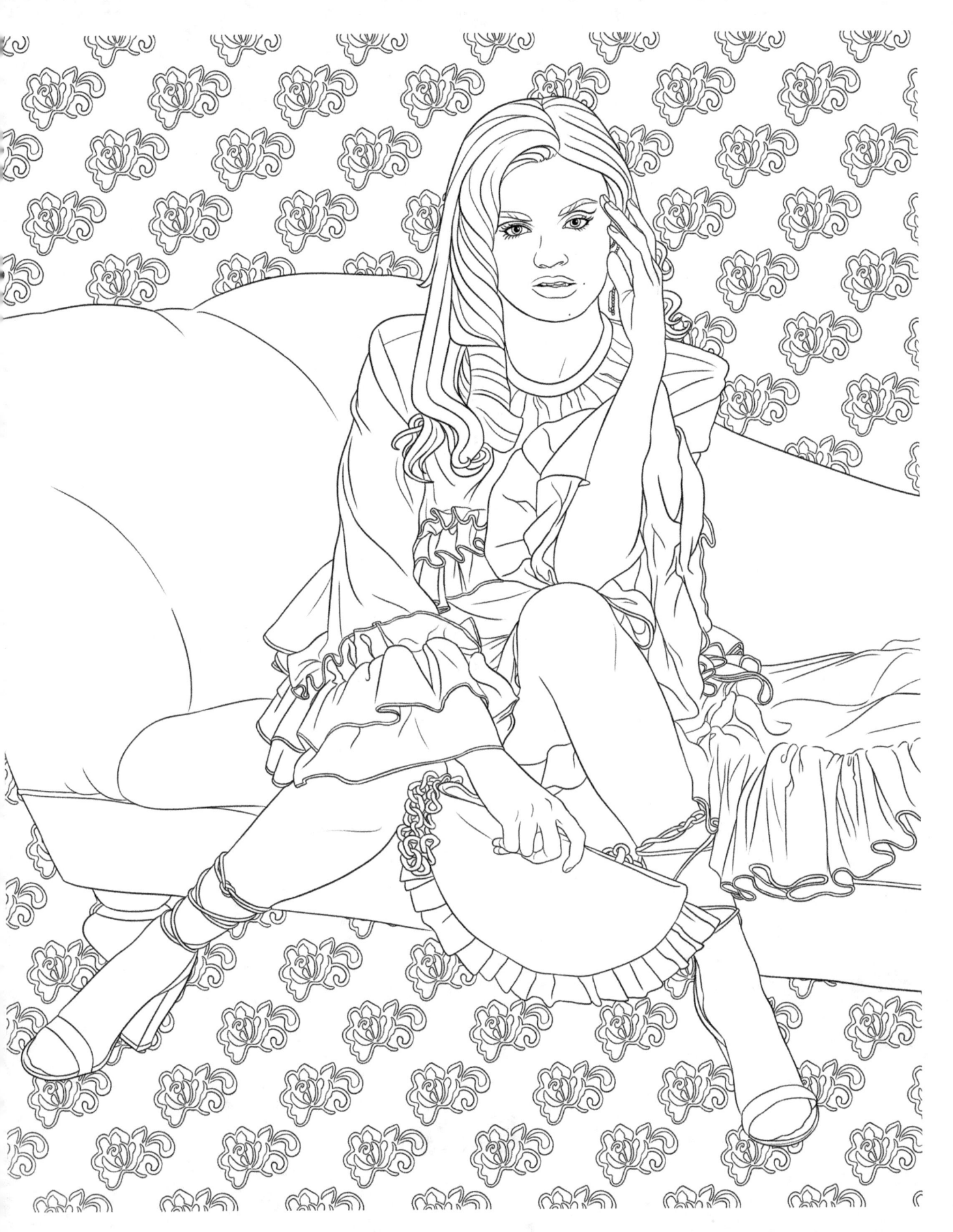

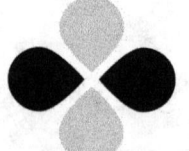

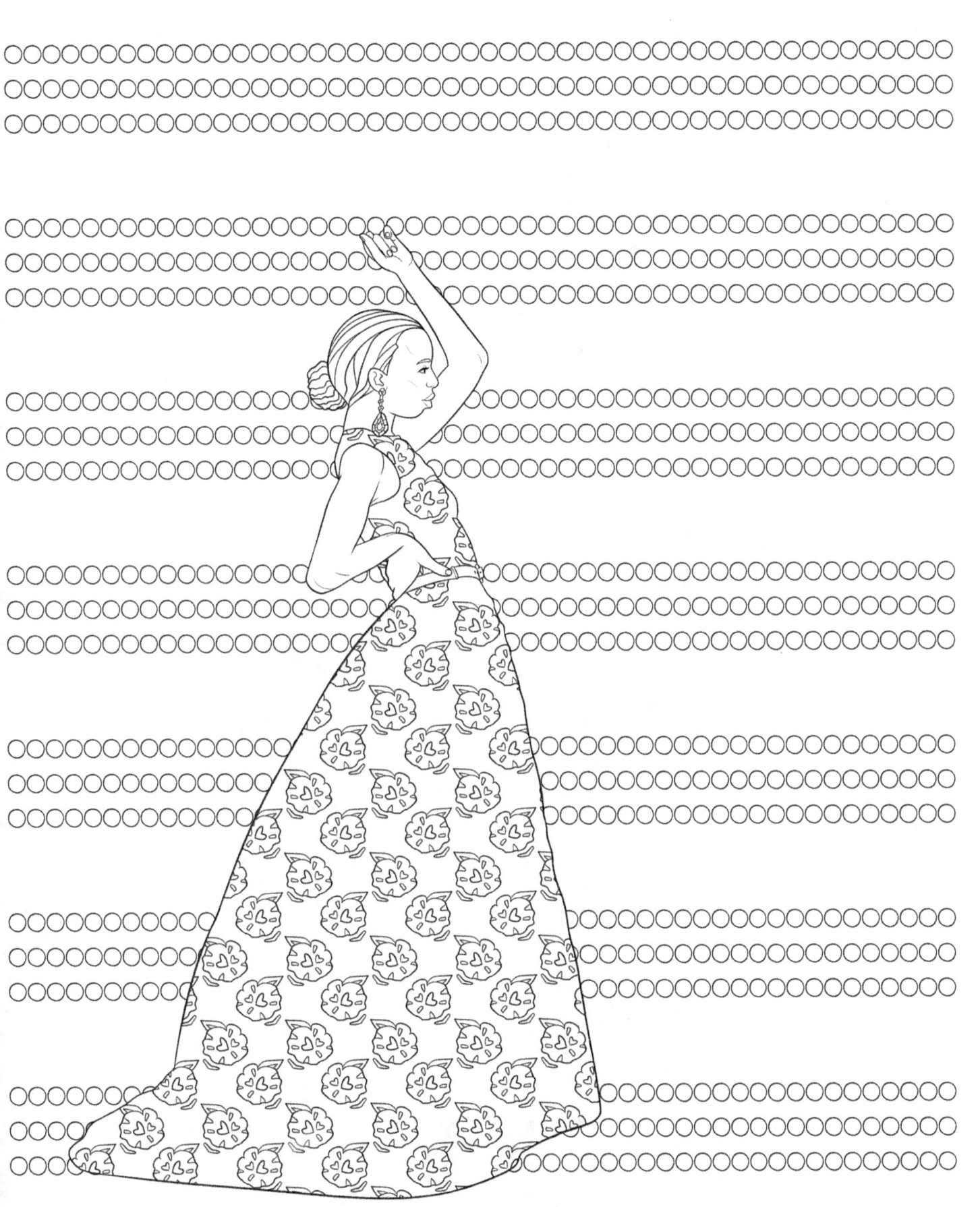

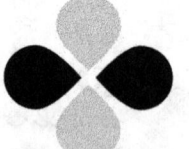

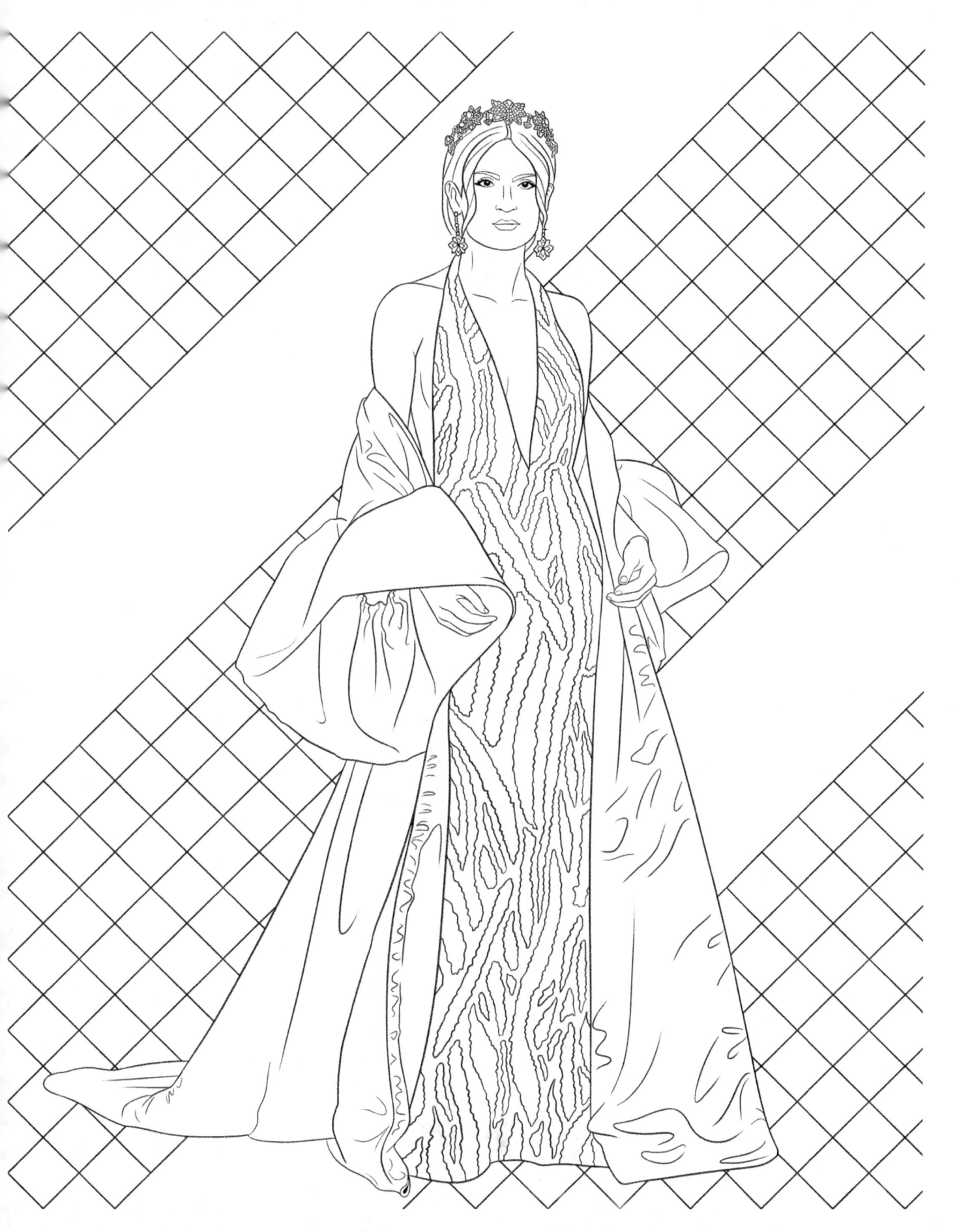

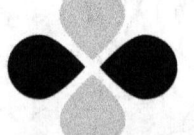

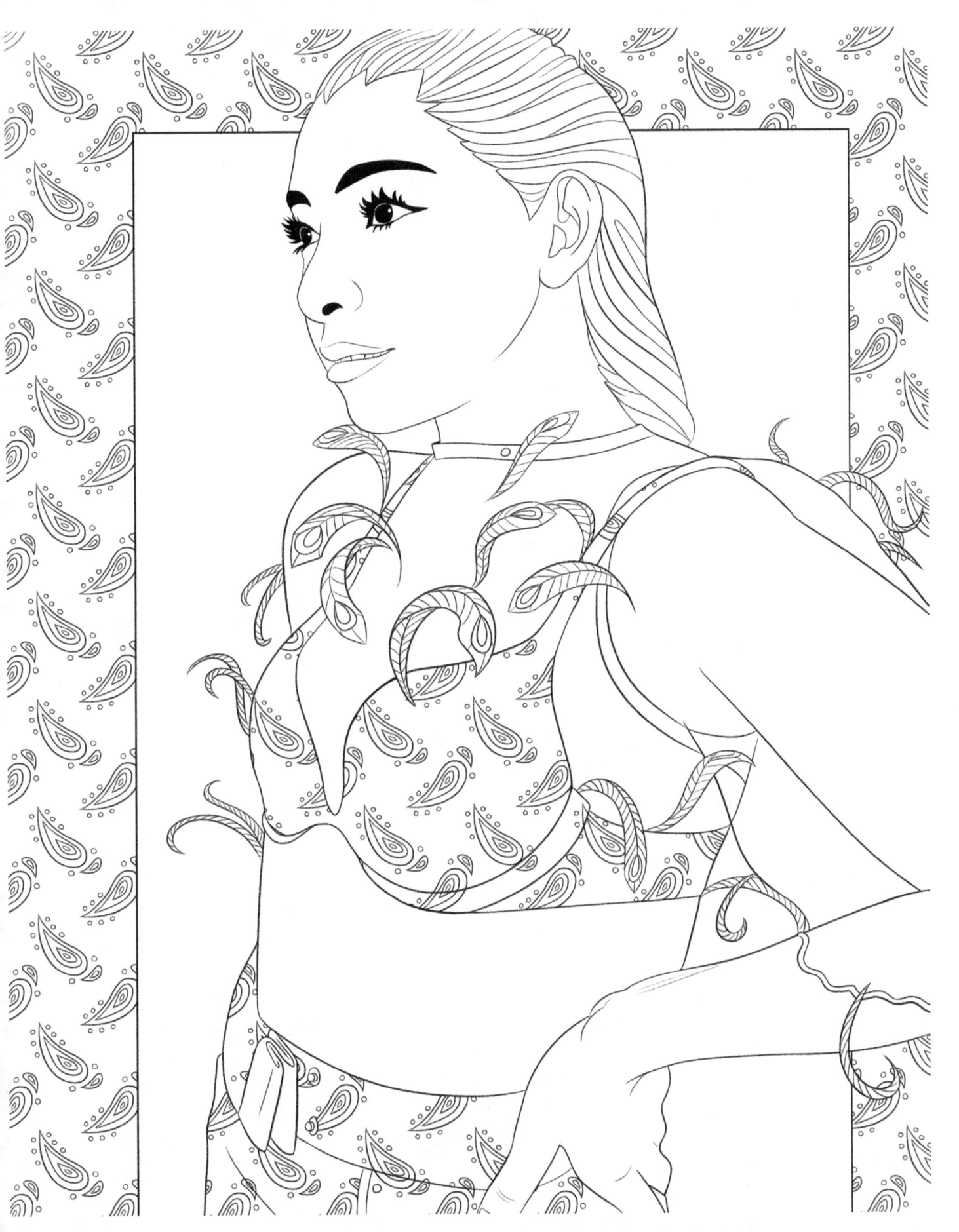

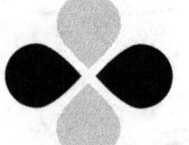

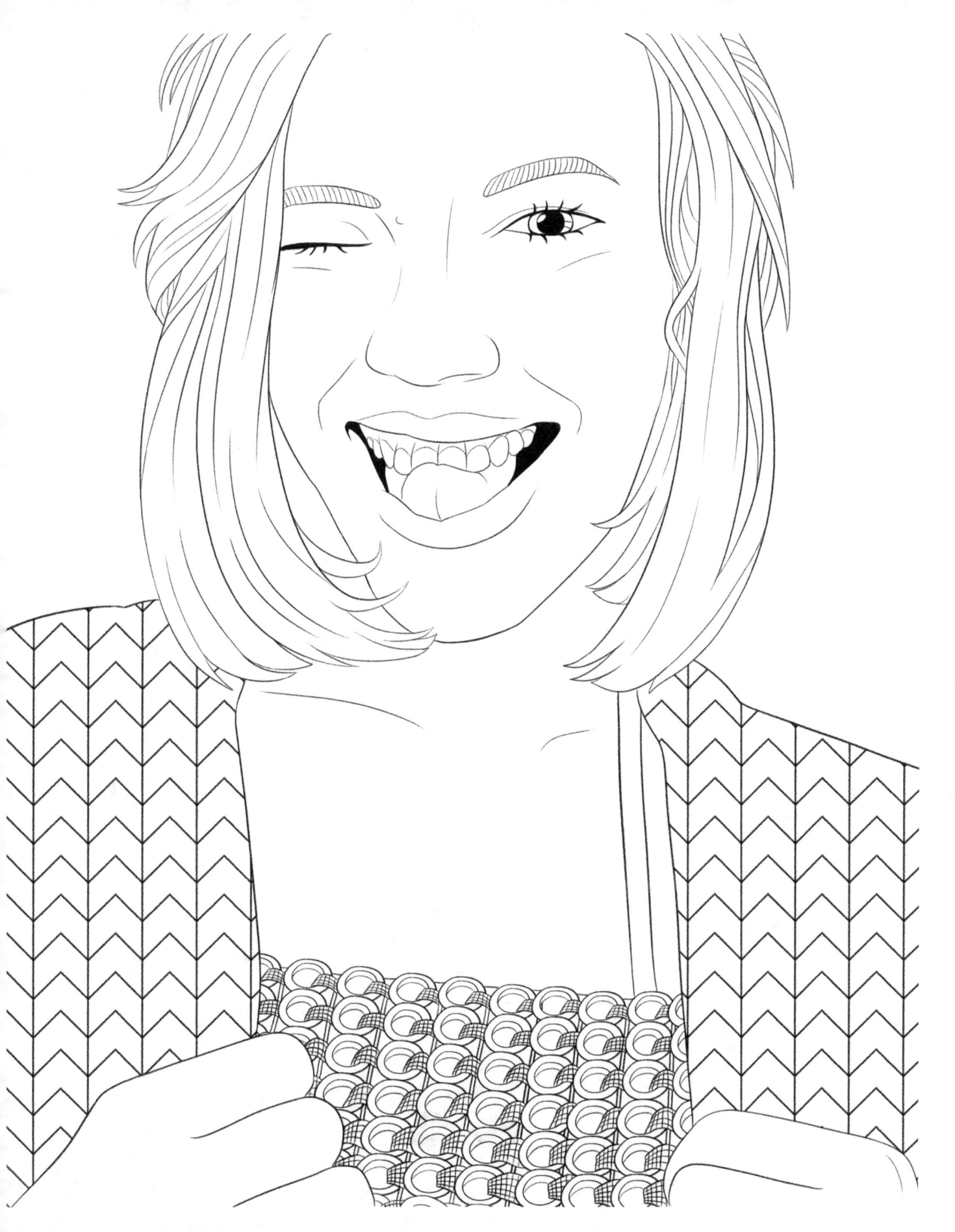

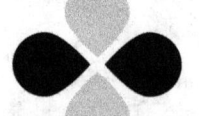

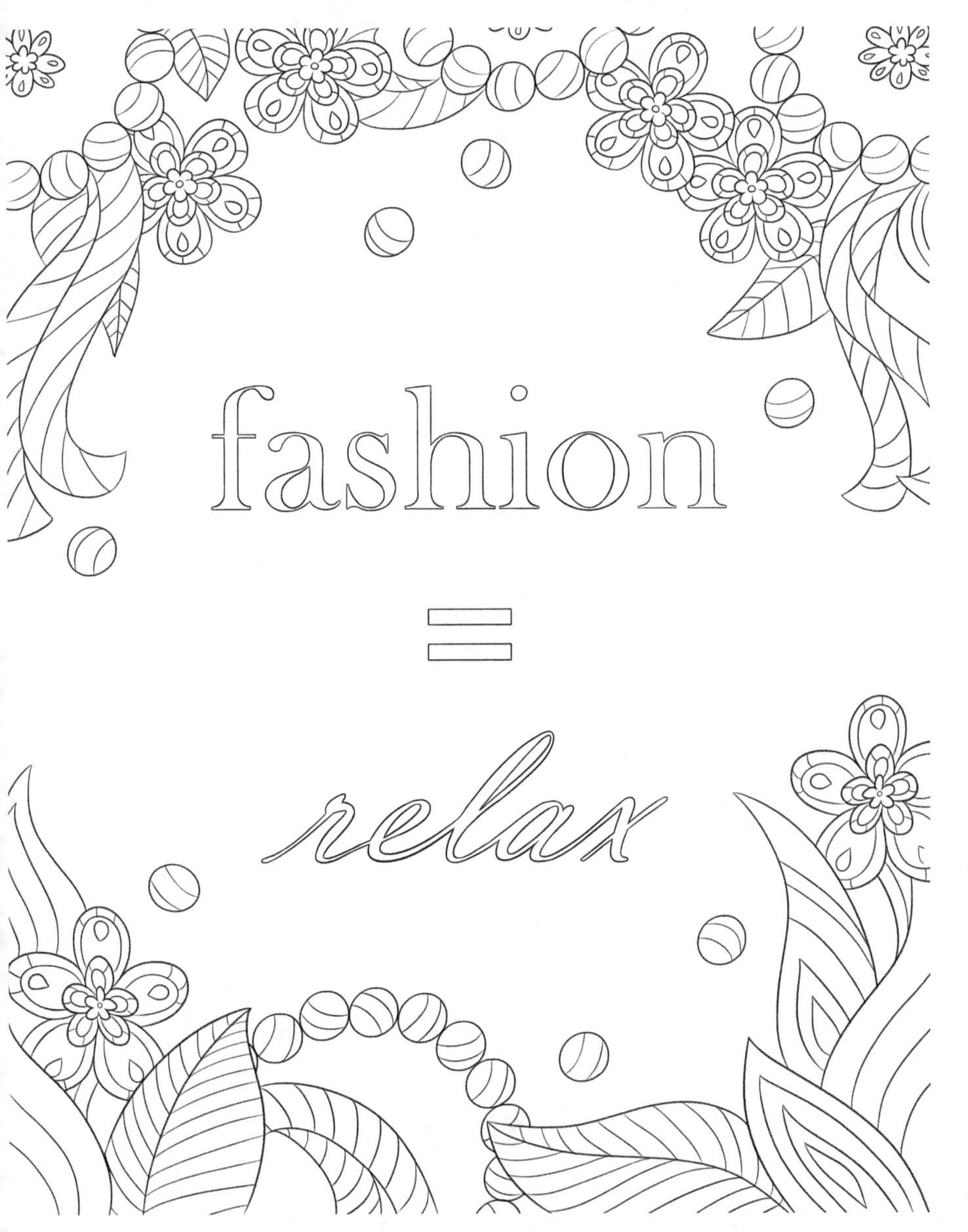

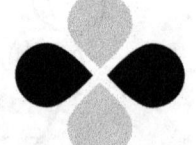

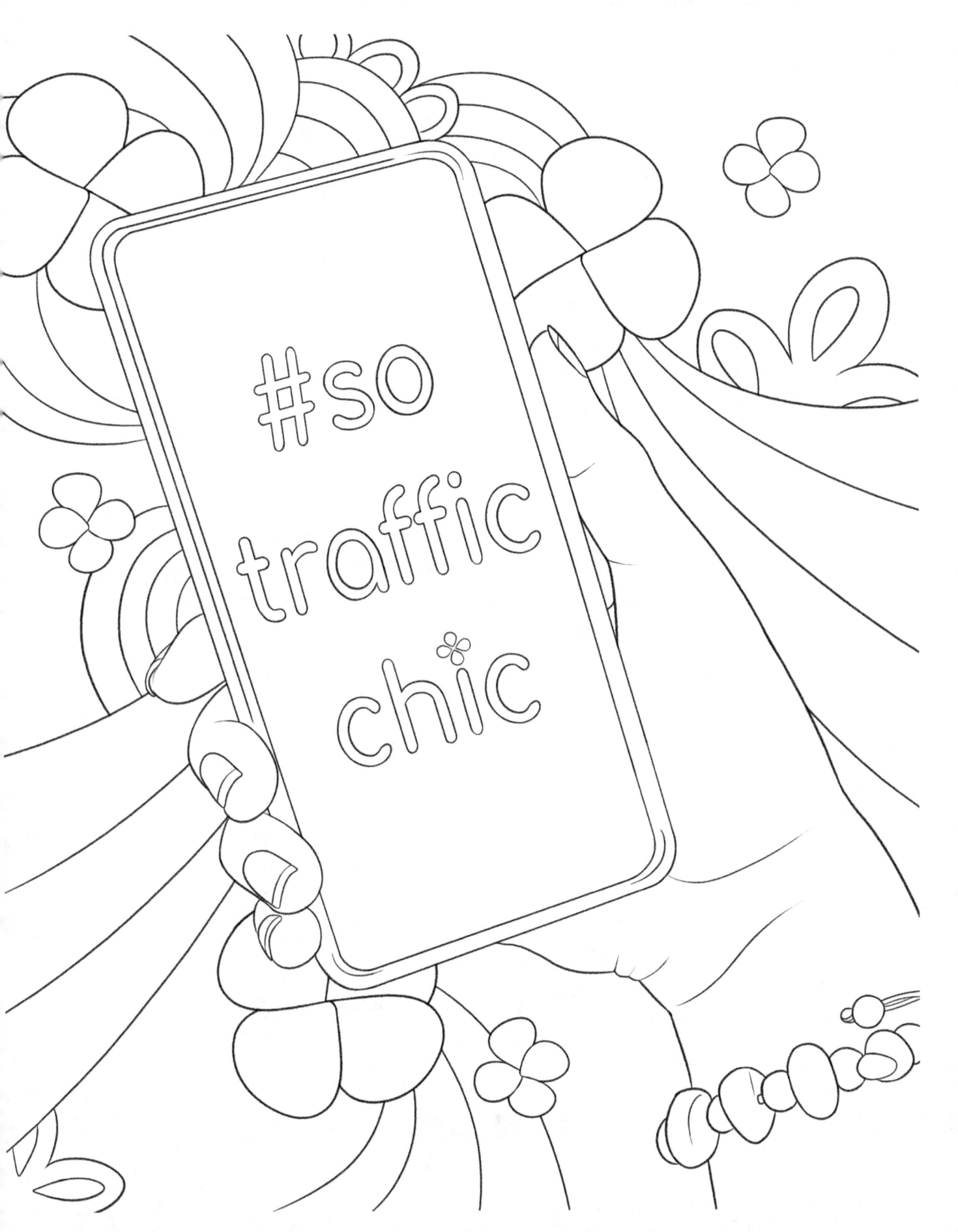

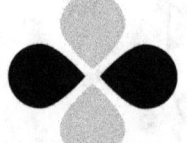

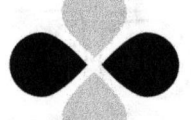

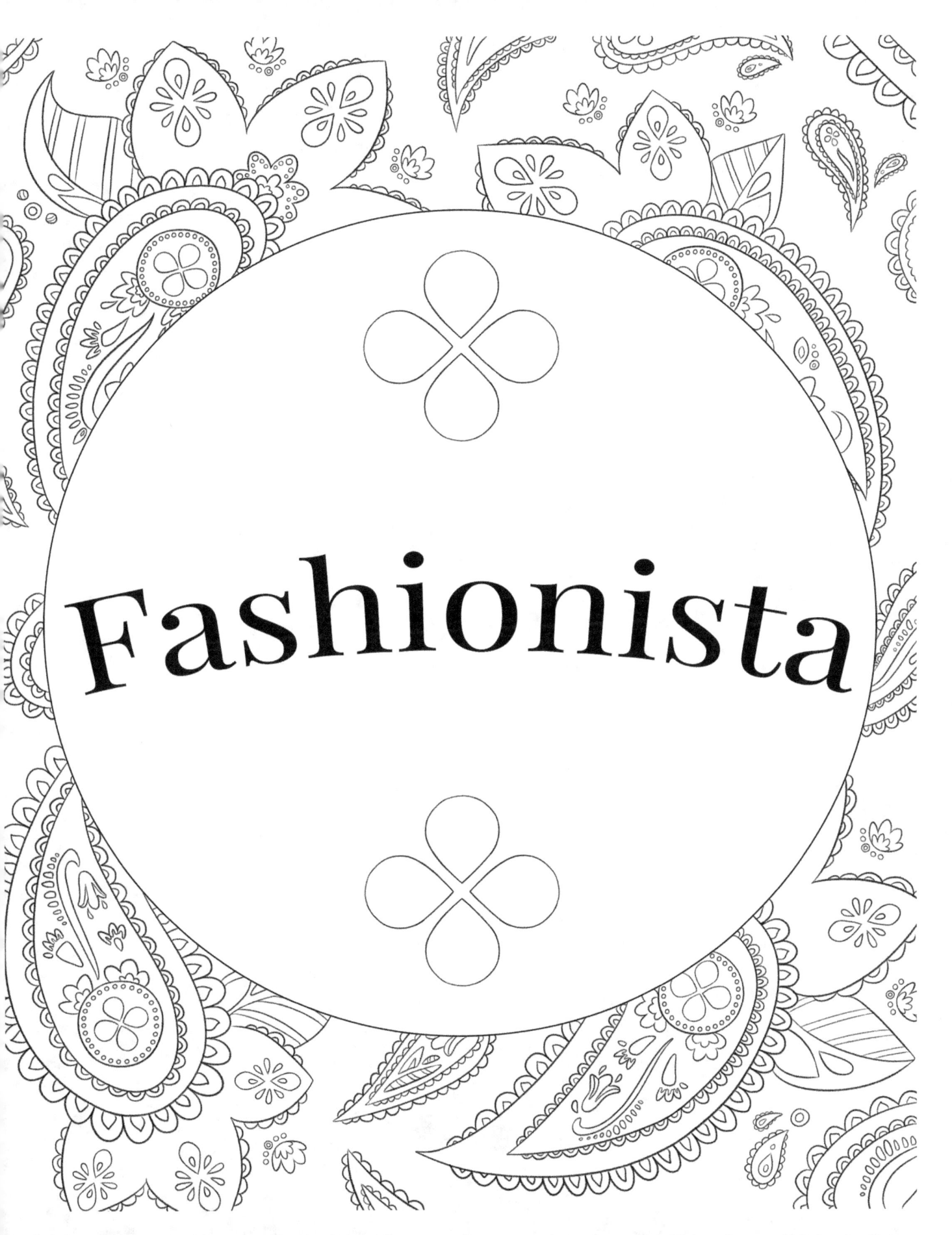

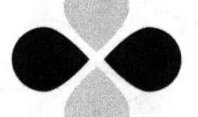

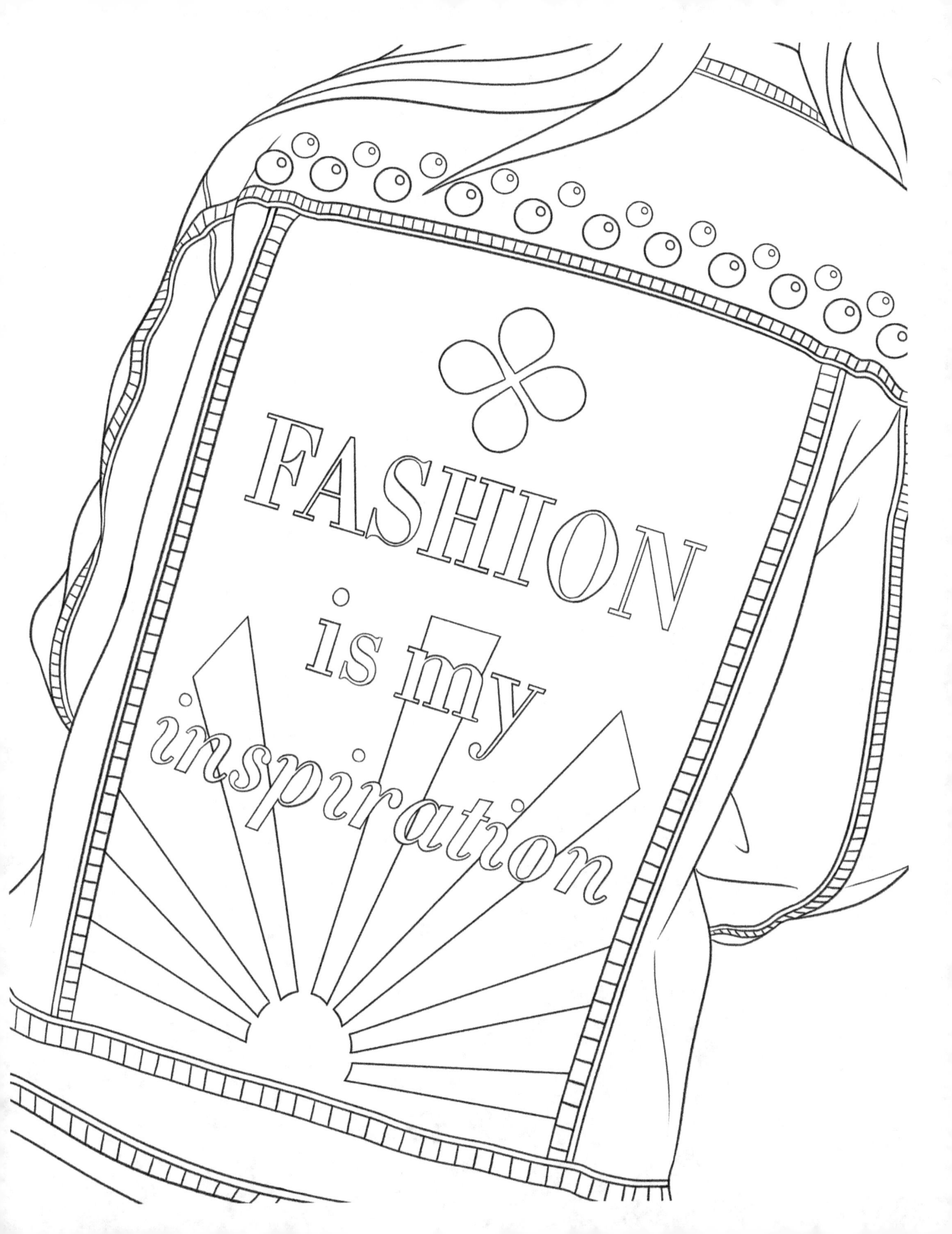

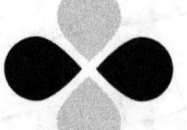

www.ingramcontent.com/pod-product-compliance
Lightning Source LLC
Chambersburg PA
CBHW081707220526
45466CB00009B/2909